25
Principles
of Reality

Jochen Blumenthal

25 Principles of Reality

© 2013 Jochen Blumenthal

ISBN 978-3-945871-84-3

Das Gesetz des Einen-Verlag (Deutschland)

Jochen Blumenthal

Bessemerstr. 82
10. OG Süd

12103 Berlin

www.dasgesetzdeseinen.de

In cooperation with L/L Research, Louisville (Kentucky)

www.llresearch.org

Contents

Preface

Dear Reader,

This little booklet contains 25 pearls of wisdom which attempt to describe in an affirmative format the one reality amongst the countless illusions: unity.

They are based on channeled material, including a portion of the Ra Contact, which Carla L. Rueckert, Don Elkins, Jim McCarty and others have received in the channeling and meditation meetings held at the premises of L/L Research in Louisville, Kentucky.

I am very grateful, to the Creator that the life work of these great souls has crossed my life, and to Carla, Jim and the L/L office (especially Gary L. Bean) who have been giving me such tremendous support in my attempt to render a service in return.

If you, dear reader, find some of the following, should we call them verses, shlokas or sutras, inspiring then my attempt was somewhat successful. If you however make yourself the gift of subsequently connecting with the unlimited universe of L/L Research's spiritual information (available at llresearch.org) you will have made it complete.

And as the Confederation teachers always say: Whatever does not vibrate with you, does not ring true to your perception of how things are, discard it. Leave it behind, alone, away – as you like. If you want, the whole booklet. You may still want to check out the L/L library though.

Love and Light, Jochen

2nd of March 2015

The Illusion of Separation

In the illusion you think
that you can only get in contact
with other beings
by using the illusion.

You express yourself in words,
send them through the air
to a telephone or whatever gadget.

This seeming separation
of one consciousness from the other
is illusion.

The separation is illusion and not reality.

The Reality of the Spiritual Worlds

Oftentimes we take

the spiritual worlds

for an illusion

and the illusion of separation

as reality.

The opposite is true.

Reality

Reality

in the first place

is the original concept

of the Creator

and not

the extensions

in form of the experiments

of His children.

The right Size of the Illusion

To gain spiritual progress
the illusion must be reduced.

This can be achieved
by taking every single facette of illusion
that is a burden to one's life,
analyzing it and then
reassigning it its proper size.

The proper size,
my friends,
is non-existence.

New Planes of Consciousness

Feel the rhythm of your breathing

as it becomes one

with everything that surrounds you.

Become aware of it.

You are in the Garden of Eden

You are in the Garden of Eden.

In this garden reigns perfection.

It provides security and protection.

Protection from all imaginable discontentment.

There is no evil in Garden Eden.

You are there when you meditate.

This place is reality.

This perfect garden is your true home.

Live this garden in your spirit.

Not just in meditation but always.

Reach out towards it, pull it near to you

and hold it closely.

Become one with your garden

because it is your true self.

Burning Desire

Desire is often misunderstood.

One doesn't pursue certain desires

for particular things.

That what desire stands for,

in reality,

is a burning fire.

The Highest Desire

Whatever you experience
is a result of your desire.
Past desires determine the present
and current desires form the seeming future.

The Creator has given to you
complete freedom of decision.
Let us give back the highest desire
which we may become aware of:

To experience the Infinite Creator
in the highest possible way.

You may be a Star

Are you aware
that you may desire
to be a star?

Are you aware,
that you may know all understandings
which you desire?

Desire under the Magnifying Glass

Desire is like the sun.

It may give heat to the earth and its inhabitants,

and provide them with light.

But if you hold a magnifying glass

into the sunbeam

you'll burn what is beneath it.

The Spiritual Nature of Creation

Man neglects

the spiritual nature of the Creation.

This a great mistake.

The Creation entirely consists

of what one would call spiritual.

There is nothing else.

The Creation is not at all

what man thinks it to be.

It only seems to him to be that way

because his consciousness is limited.

Free Will

The truth
of the love of the Creator
needs to develop from inside.

It can not be imposed from outside.

The Plan of the Creator

Desire is the key

to that which you receive.

What you desire

you'll receive.

This is the plan of the Creator.

Reduce the Illusion

Reduce

through meditation

the illusion of seeming separation.

Man has fabricated it himself.

The Living Creation

The Creation is alive.

It is intelligent

and functions as one being.

You are part of it,

a being,

that breathes the air of Eternity.

Isolated Parts

Some parts of the Creator
have isolated themselves.
They have moved away from
the original thought of the Creator.

Man, too,
through his experiences and experiments
has become isolated
in his thinking.

A very Important Desire

Take care of the desire

to seek and find

outside of the material illusion

that has dominated this planet so many years.

Unlimited

The universe is unlimited.

For your identity,

your journey of seeking,

your understanding of the Creation,

there is no end.

Unity

What is unlimited
can not be many.
Manyness is limited.
Infinity is unified.
In an unlimited Creator
there is nothing except unity.

Love and Light and Light and Love

In truth,

there is no right or wrong.

The opposites will be reunified.

You are everything,

every being,

every emotion,

everything that happens,

every situation.

You are unity. You are infinity.

You are Love and Light, Light and Love.

The Truth of the Love of the Creator

Every being

needs to be able

to accept or refuse

what is of aid

for one's spiritual development.

Only in this way

the truth of the Creator,

who is the Creation,

the truth of the love of the Creator,

may be realized.

Complicated Illusion

Man himself

has created this illusion

through his complexity.

Release the complications.

Become aware of what

has created you.

The Desire of the Creator

Become aware of the Creator.

Become aware of His desires.

Then you'll know yours.

Because you and the Creator,

you are one.

You will feel it

when you became aware of His desires.

There will be no more questions.

You will have found what you are looking for.

You will have found love.

This is the desire of the Creator.

Find the Love of the Creator

Express the love of the Creator

which created you.

Find it in meditation.

No intellectual effort,

no careful planning,

no interpretation of spoken or written words

will lead you to that simple truth.

A Thought of Love

Become capable of understanding
the qualities of the possibilities
of the illusion.

React
through introspection and meditation
in a way that expresses
the thought of the Creator:
with a thought of love.

Key terms

Term	Text
Consciousness	1, 5, 9, 11, 22
Creator, Creation	3, 11, 12, 13, 15, 16, 18, 19, 21, 23, 24, 25
Eternal, infinite	15, 18, 19, 20
Free Will	8, 12, 21
Identity, being	6, 12, 18, 25
Illusion	1, 2, 4, 14, 17, 22, 25
Life, vitality	4, 15
Love and Light	10, 12, 20, 21, 23, 24, 25
Sun, Logos, universe	9, 10, 18
Spirituality, meditation	4, 6, 11, 14, 18, 21, 23, 24, 25
Thought, thinking	6, 16, 25
Unity	5, 6, 19, 20, 23
Wisdom, knowing, intelligence	6, 9, 12, 15, 18, 21, 23, 24, 25

References

Derived from transmissions channeled by Carla Rueckert and others at L/L Research

01 – 04	Hatonn, 28th May 1974
05	Oxal, 8th April 1974
06	Hatonn, 10th April 1974
07 – 11	Hatonn, 12th April 1974
12	unknown
13, 22-24	Hatonn, 31st Mai 1974
18 – 20	Ra 1.7, 15th January 1981
21 – 25	unknown

About the author

Jochen Blumenthal, born 1976 near the Lake of Constance, is the German translator of the Ra Contact. In 2014 he started up the *Das Gesetz des Einen*-Verlag (Deutschland) publishing house to provide more of L/L Research's material in German and other languages.

Jochen has studied and worked in several fields including anthropology, political sciences, business administration and spirituality. Concluding that L/L Research's channeled information is among the most important for humanity he devotes himself to translating and publishing this information further.

Additional information

The "*Das Gesetz des Einen*-Verlag (Deutschland)" publishing house offers a small range of own derivative English publications since L/L Research provides all of their channeled information, and a growing number of great books, to English speaking readers.

All of L/L Research's resources are freely available online and can be purchased at the L/L online store.

Among the works of L/L Research are

- *The Ra-Contact: Teaching the Law of One*
- *Living the Law of One, 101: The Choice*
- *A Wanderer's Handbook*
- *Channelings from the Holy Spirit*
- *Secrets of the UFO*
- *Tilting at Windmills*

L/L Research's internet address is www.llresearch,org.

The "*Das Gesetz des Einen*-Verlag (Germany)" satellite

The "*Das Gesetz des Einen*-Verlag (Deutschland)" offers a growing number of translations and derivative and explanatory works based on L/L Research material. In cooperation with the Belgian translator Micheline Deschreider, and under the name "Maison d'édition La Loi Une (Allemagne)", it also offers French versions of L/L Research's and own derivative works.

Among the publications are:

In German:

- *Der Ra-Kontakt: Das Gesetz des Einen lehren*
- *25 Prinzipien der Realität*
- *Meditation*
- *Lehrmeister Jesus*
- *Dienst der Liebe*
- *Bündnisbotschaften Sammelband*
- *Essenz I*

- *Außerirdische Kommunikation*
- *Das Gesetz des Einen leben, Das 1x1: Die Wahl* (Teil I & II)

In French:

- *Le contact Ra: La Loi Une enseignée*
- *Comment vivre la Loi Une, Niveau I: Le Choix*
- *Vade mecum du pèlerin errant*
- *25 principes de réalité*
- *Méditation*
- *Service d'Amour*
- *Jésus, Le Maître Enseignant*

In Dutch & Swedish:

- *25 Principes van de realiteit* (Coen Weesjes)
- *Kosmiska principer: 25 principer om verkligheten* (Translation by Klas Häger)

www.ingramcontent.com/pod-product-compliance
Lightning Source LLC
Chambersburg PA
CBHW060546030426
42337CB00021B/4452